ABE FUNK

HOPE

FOR THE SMALL CHURCH

Essence
PUBLISHING

Belleville, Ontario, Canada

Library and Archives Canada Cataloguing in Publication

Funk, Abe, 1936-
    Hope for the small church / Abe Funk.

Includes bibliographical references.
ISBN 1-55306-985-4

    1. Small churches. 2. Rural churches. 3. Christian leadership. I. Title.

BV637.8.F85 2005   254'.24   C2005-904926-X

For more information or
to order additional copies, please contact:

Abe Funk
27—308 Jackson Road NW
Edmonton, AB T6L 6W1

Essence Publishing is a Christian Book Publisher dedicated to furthering the work of Christ through the written word. For more information, contact: 20 Hanna Court, Belleville, Ontario, Canada K8P 5J2.
Phone: 1-800-238-6376. Fax: (613) 962-3055.
E-mail: publishing@essencegroup.com
Internet: www.essencegroup.com

Printed in Canada
by

Essence
PUBLISHING

Table of Contents

Keep watch over yourselves and all the flock of which the Holy Spirit has made you overseers. Be shepherds of the church of God, which he bought with his own blood.

ACTS 20:28

Introduction

While good books have been written about and for the town and country church, or the small church, few deal with the everyday, internal leadership issues of these congregations. My goal is to specifically help the boards of these churches. Many of the things I deal with here would not be of interest to the average church member, as they are specifically written for small church boards.

Many small churches struggle with the basic issues of leadership. My desire is to give them hope and help them become healthy and effective. I believe that many small churches can be revitalized through leadership development.

I grew up in a farming community in southern Saskatchewan. I had my start in a little Sunday school on the corner of my parents' yard. Later we attended church in our small town of a few hundred people. It was there where I was first given the opportunity to be involved in ministry. I taught my first Sunday school class, led a choir and preached my first sermon. My first pastorate was in a small town in Minnesota.

When I began ministry as a District Minister, someone suggested that I take a Lyle Schaller seminar. He helped me to understand the town and country church. He helped me to appreciate the small church. He set me on a path to encourage and help them.

During more than thirty years in denominational work, I have always had a concern for our smaller churches. To me, size is not an issue, but health and effectiveness are important. Small churches in small places can have effective ministries. Many are bogged down with traditions that are no longer relevant, or they are stuck in one form of conflict or another.

It is my hope and prayer that this manual will encourage smaller congregations to be the best that they can be for the Kingdom of God in their communities. The spiritual needs of rural communities are growing every day. There is still a lot of good ministry to be done in these communities. It is important that we keep a witness for the gospel in every community.

I dedicate this manual to the many faithful leaders who work hard to make their churches shining lights in their communities.

ABE FUNK D. D.
Edmonton, Alberta

How to Use This Book

Finding time when busy people can come together for training is always challenging. I have therefore designed this manual to be used for half-hour training sessions at the start of each board meeting. If you are afraid of adding an additional half-hour to an already too-long meeting, don't worry; you'll get better at doing board. The time invested in training will only enhance your meetings.

Most board members come with little preparation for the important task of leading a church. One reason many good people are reluctant to join leadership teams is that they don't feel qualified. Others don't see it as a significant enough challenge. A continuing training program will sharpen their skills and raise their levels of performance and satisfaction.

I suggest that each leader have a copy of this book as their personal manual. That way they can underline and make notes in the margin and in the space provided. It's intended to be a workbook, not just another book to read and to be stuck on a dusty shelf. The more this book is marked up and used, the happier the author will be.

Perhaps leaders can take turns presenting lessons. The sixteen lessons have come out of issues that I see as challenges in many small churches. Over a year and a half of leadership meetings, you will cover many of the challenges facing small churches. If someone takes notes of your discussions, you can add your own material to this manual for your future training sessions.

Don't stop with this book. Keep on learning and growing as leaders. I have seen struggling churches grow to health and effectiveness by developing their leaders. Trained leaders will set the pace for a healthy new direction for your church.

I pray that you will continue to *"grow in the grace and knowledge of our Lord and Savior Jesus Christ"* (2 Peter 3:18). Keep growing in your leadership skills.

Don't stop with this book. Keep on learning and growing as leaders....Keep growing in your leadership skills.

"God's first concern is not what the church
does, it is what the church is."

RAY STEDMAN

"To live above with saints we love,
that will be glory. But to live below with saints
we know, well, that's another story."

AUTHOR UNKNOWN

"Being included in God's family is
the highest honour and the greatest privilege
you will ever receive."

RICK WARREN

The church needs you and
you need the church.

LESSON ONE

Let's First Think About the Church

"It is my conviction that a fresh understanding of the biblical doctrine of the church practically related to our daily, corporate activities as Christians, can and will give a new sense of purpose and direction to our Christian lives."

– MICHAEL GRIFFITHS

READ: ROMANS 11:33-12:8

I have given forty-seven years to serving the Lord and His church. I still marvel that He gave me that great responsibility. What a wonderful privilege and honour it has been. Not that it has always been easy. I have seen churches at their worst. Let's be honest about it; we are all sinners and broken in many ways. I have seen churches hurt a lot of people. Many individuals have become disillusioned by the failings of the church. I could make my own long list, as you could, too, I'm sure. So why do I still continue serving the church well past my retirement? It's because I believe that the church is still God's best plan and the only hope for the world. As long as God gives me the strength, I will give myself to encouraging and serving His church and its leaders.

Before we learn about leadership in the church, let's explore what the church really is. We need to understand the nature of the church.

People see the church as many different things. To some, it is a social organization that brings people together for fellowship. Others see the church as caring for the needs of people. Some see the church as a political organization vying for rights and lobbying for reforms in the community. For some, it stands as a symbol of worship and righteousness. All these perceptions and expectations are good and are what the church may do, but what really is the church?

The church is not just another organization with other organizations in our community. The church is God's institution, yet more than an institution. Built by Jesus Christ, it is His body in the world today. The church is God's presence in this world.

The New Testament presents the church on two levels, the universal church worldwide and the local congregation. The primary emphasis is on the local church. Of the 112 references to the church, only twelve refer to the universal church. The universal church makes us one with all believers of all time everywhere. The local church is that group of believers that we meet with for worship, edification and ministry.

When someone says, "Oh, I am just a member of the universal church," that may sound lofty, but it's usually an excuse for lack of commitment. "How do I get involved?" "Where do I give my tithe?" "Who will call on me if I get sick?" The universal church is a wonderful reality, but for practical Christianity, you must be a part of, and be active in, a local company of believers.

The local church, whatever its size, is where public worship takes place. It is there where we are taught the rich truths of God's Word. It is in and through the local church that primary spiritual growth happens. It is in the local church that we are meant to be cared for when we get wounded. It is in the local church that we are corrected and restored when we stray. It is through the local church that we serve our community and our world as light and salt.

The most basic definition of the church is what Jesus said in Matthew 18:20: *"Where two or three come together in my name, there am I with them."* He chose twelve to make up the first core of believers. There were 120 in the upper room waiting for the promise of the Holy Spirit. After that, there were thousands. So it doesn't matter what size your church may be, the important thing is that it is a church in New Testament terms, healthy and effective.

There are many pictures of the church in the New Testament:

- The bride of Christ (Revelation 19:7);
- A building (Ephesians 2:19-22);
- The priesthood (1 Peter 2:5-9);
- The flock (John 10:1-18);
- Branches and the Vine (John 15); and
- The body (Romans 12:5).

Each picture gives us a different view of the rich relationship that we have in Jesus Christ and with each other. No one picture is complete in itself. Even all of them together fall short in some way to fully describe the wonder and marvel of God living in His people.

Requirements for membership in the church are simply repentance, baptism and continuing in the Apostles' teaching (Acts 2:38-41).

The purpose of the church is to bring believers to maturity so that they will be witnesses for Christ and bring the good news to their Jerusalem, their Judea, their Samaria and to the ends of the earth (Matthew 28:18-20). We glorify God when we live out His teachings.

My pastor often reminds us that the church is the only hope for our troubled world. All other institutions and schemes have failed and are failing. But the church is the hope for the future. The church has the power of the Holy Spirit to effect real change in the lives of people. What a great privilege we have of being a part of serving the Lord and His church in a time like this.

Of all the chapters in this book, this is by far the most important one. If you are going to provide leadership in His church, then it is important that you know what the church is and what God wants His church to be and do. I encourage you, if you are a leader in your church, to learn all you can about the church and God's plan for the church. It will give you the perspective that you will need in your leadership. It will help you to stay focused and to not become discouraged.

I encourage you to continue your study of the church.

TALK ABOUT THIS:

- What has been your experience with the church?
- Is there a need for you to learn more about the church?

- Do you understand the pulse and needs of your church?

NOW PRAY:

Thank God for the church and for the privilege of being a part of His body. Ask God to help you, the leaders of the church, to lead your church to health and effectiveness.

MY NOTES:

In a big world, the small church has remained
INTIMATE.

In a fast world, the small church has been
STEADY.

In a complex world, the small church has remained
SIMPLE.

In a rational world, the small church has kept
FEELING.

In a mobile world, the small church has been an
ANCHOR.

In an anonymous world, the small church
CALLS US BY NAME

CARL S. DUDLEY

LESSON TWO

Town and Country Churches—
What Are They Like?

*One half of the churches in Canada have fewer
than seventy-five people in worship. In the US,
the average church attracts fewer than ninety
on a weekend. Many have fewer than fifty
in worship. Only 2 percent of churches
have more than 1,000 people.*

READ: MATTHEW 9:35-38; ACTS 16:11-15

*My first pastorate was in a small town in Minnesota. The
church had been closed for two years because of internal
conflict. Wanting to give it "another try," as they put it,
the church of about twenty-five people invited my new
bride and me to be their pastor. In my youthful enthu-
siasm, I looked for ways to reach the community. Most
people claimed to attend church; at least they knew the
church they did not attend regularly. I visited the entire
community. No one was interested in attending my little*

church. Finally we tried a program for children and young people—a hobby club in winter and a recreation program in the summer. It was the door that opened the community to the church. Forty-seven years later, that church still has an effective ministry in the community.

Lyle Schaller, in his book, *The Small Church is Different*, writes, "The facts suggest that the natural size of the worshipping congregation is that of the small church." He says that churches can be grown larger but that it is like pumping water uphill: the harder you pump, the bigger the church you can grow. He also states that, "The large church is not an enlarged version of the small congregation, and the small-membership church is not a miniature replica of the big church." They are different. How are they different?

- Town and country churches are tough;
- They are built around family and friendship relationships;
- They are more concerned about people than about excellence;
- They are primarily voluntary organizations;
- The grapevine can be used as an asset;
- They are intergenerational;
- They have a place for everyone;
- Meetings tend to be dominated by social activities; and
- Boards tend to do less in favour of including everyone.

We must accept the realities of the town and country churches. They are different than larger, city churches. Their potential and growth may be limited. Sometimes they are in declining communities.

There is, however, still a lot of good ministry to be done in rural communities, providing that churches can think creatively and are open to change.

Most resources are geared to larger churches. Town- and country-church leaders need to be selective in choosing resources. They need to translate what they learn into their own situation and not just transfer programs from other churches into their ministry.

The inner state and health of a church is more telling about its potential than the influences it has on the outside in the community. Healthy churches will find ways to be effective witnesses in their communities.

The longer we have lived in a community, the more blind spots we tend to have. If you have not recently done it, you should do a thorough community assessment. You may be surprised by what you learn. You may find people who you have overlooked. I am amazed how often church leaders say, "I thought I knew my community," after doing such a study.

Every church can find a way to be "salt" and "light" in their community.

Talk About This:

- Describe your community. What is the story here?
- What are your church's greatest strengths?
- How does your church differ from other churches?
- What should you be exploring?

Now Pray:

Ask God to help you understand your community and your church and to give you a deep love for both of them.

MY NOTES:

"The facts suggest that the natural size of the worshipping congregation is that of the small church."

LYLE SCHALLER

"Every church is unmistakably unique."

CHRISTIAN A. SCHWARZ

Each church has a special mission to fulfill.

Healthy churches are growing churches.

LESSON THREE

What Does a Healthy Church Look Like?

The size of a church is not important. What is important is that a church is healthy and fulfilling the mission to which God has called it.

READ: EPHESIANS 4:1-16

"What our church needs is some old-time fire-and-brimstone preaching. That's what we got when I was growing up here, and the church was full," argued Bill.

"I disagree," added Jerry. "Times have changed, and people don't respond in the same way today. I think the secret in reaching our community lies with us, the members. I think the tension we have had here recently is keeping people away."

"I wonder," Pastor Dave added thoughtfully, "if we

should take a look at the bigger picture of our church and our community. Instead of looking for a quick fix, we should rather do an overall evaluation of who we are today and why we are here."

How can these leaders decide what a healthy church looks like? Is it a busy church? Is it sound doctrinally? Is it concerned only about its membership, or does it also care for people in the community?

Christian A. Schwarz, author of *The ABCs of Natural Church Development*, has identified eight characteristics generally considered to be signs of a healthy church. They are:

- *Empowering Leadership*: Leaders who are not only leading but also preparing others to lead in their place;
- *Gift-Oriented Ministry*: Every member of the body of Christ serving in the ways that the Spirit of God has gifted them to serve;
- *Passionate Spirituality*: Prayerful, enthusiastic, bold and curious about knowing, loving and serving God in this church with a sense of commitment;
- *Functional Structures*: Having in place the structures to accomplish God's vision of the church in our society;
- *Inspiring Worship Services*: Is going to church fun, or a duty?
- *Holistic Small Groups*: Going beyond the consideration of a passage of Scripture to meeting the genuine needs of the participants;
- *Need-Oriented Evangelism*: Evangelism that focuses on the agenda of the lost, not the niceties of one's preferences; and

- *Loving Relationships*: A high quotient of the relationships measured in time and effort invested in each other. When was the last time you spent significant time with a person from your congregation apart from regular church?

On the other hand, what does an unhealthy church look like?

- It has become blind to the needs of people around it;
- It becomes unwilling to adapt to a changing community;
- It has become spiritually lukewarm; the passion and fire have faded;
- Its fellowship becomes ingrown and self-centered;
- It has spiritual malnutrition—it is not well fed on the Word of God;
- It has head knowledge, but daily life does not measure up;
- Its leadership lacks vision, purpose and direction; and
- There are ongoing, unresolved conflicts.

It is a realistic expectation that each church becomes healthy and effective, making progress in fulfilling its mission. Size is not the important factor. Portraying a Christ-like spirit and producing the fruit of the Spirit are signs of a healthy church. A church that is not reaching out to its community, has not seen a person come to faith in Christ or baptized people for some time is not a very healthy church. There have to be signs of life. Some churches have been dysfunctional for so long that unhealthy behaviour begins to look normal.

Many churches that have the potential to grow don't, because either they don't understand growth principles or they're not willing to change sufficiently to let the growth happen. Growth is change, and bigger is different. The leadership of the church needs to stay alert to the changing needs and characteristics of the community and the congregation.

TALK ABOUT THIS:

- Which characteristics of a healthy church describe your church?
- Do you show any traits of an unhealthy church?
- How could you build on your strengths?
- How could you strengthen a weakness?

NOW PRAY:

Ask the Lord of the church to help you to understand your church and help it to move forward to health and effectiveness.

MY NOTES:

Some churches have been dysfunctional for so long that unhealthy behaviour begins to look normal.

"Our greatest challenge as leaders is to
develop a godly character."

J. ROBERT CLINTON

"The more positive qualities you are going to
look for the more you are going to find."

JOHN C. MAXWELL

Jesus did not ask for volunteers.
He handpicked His team.

Build a team to complement your weaknesses

LESSON FOUR

Building Your Leadership Team

Choosing the right people to serve on the leadership team is the most important issue facing many churches. Jesus spent a night in prayer before He chose His dream team.

READ: LUKE 6:12-16; 1 TIMOTHY 3:8-13

To prepare for his journey to the South Pole, Sir Ernest Shackleton placed the following ad: "Men wanted for hazardous journey. Small wages, bitter cold, long months of complete darkness, constant danger. Safe return doubtful." *Five thousand applied, many of them highly professional people. He selected about thirty to form his crew. It sounds familiar to Jesus' call in Matthew 16:24:* "If anyone would come after me, he must deny himself and take up his cross and follow me."

There is no greater recruiting story than the story you have just read in Luke 6. Jesus had a slight advantage over us in seeing the potential and choosing the right people. Look at the twelve He chose. They were very ordinary people. They had little education. They were certainly not from the cultured elite of the community. All except Judas were from the backcountry of Galilee. The group consisted of fishermen, a tax collector with questionable credentials, a freedom fighter and some name-only followers. Few would have given them much serious thought. Yet in only three years with the Master, they were accused of turning the world upside-down (Acts 17:6 KJV).

A great leadership team begins with a leader. Leaders have to model what they want to happen on their team. That is called self-leadership. To grow a team, we first have to grow ourselves. Jesus was that model leader, building a team unequalled in history.

We will never measure up to Jesus' abilities, but the life He lived and the principles He taught apply to us who are leaders today. He is our model leader.

Jesus knew what kind of team He would need. What was He looking for when He called those twelve men to follow Him? His call was simple enough: "Follow Me," was all He asked. Be with Me. Watch what I do and imitate Me. "Become like Me," was His call. It sounds simple enough, but there is enough in that call for a lifetime of learning.

By raising the standard, you will attract a higher-quality leader. Good people don't want to commit to mediocrity.

The first qualification we look for in building a leadership team is character. Is this person true to his word? Is he dependable? Is he a team player? Does he live what he professes? Do his peers respect him?

A potential board member needs to be an example of a growing Christian. No one is perfect, but potential leaders need to be growing people. The followers of Jesus were anything but perfect, but they followed and they grew in the process. Paul put it this way in 1 Timothy 3:2: *"Now an overseer must be above reproach."* He then lists other qualities in verses 1-13, but character tops the list.

When looking for new leaders, you want to find people who are regular in worship, regular with Bible study and prayer, who tithe their income, are team players and have a servant's heart.

TALK ABOUT THIS:

- What were the disciples like when Jesus first called them?
- How can you grow and develop further as a leadership team?
- How can you continue to build your future dream team?

NOW PRAY:

Pray for each other that you will be known as leaders of character and that you will be aware of new people you need to encourage to become part of your leadership team in the future.

MY NOTES:

As long as you're green, you're growing. As soon as you think you're ripe, you start to rot.

For a church to be healthy, it needs qualified growing leaders.

There is no shortcut to quality.

"Blessed are your eyes because they see, and your ears because they hear."

MATTHEW 13:16

LESSON FIVE

Training Your Dream Team

*Our usefulness increases when we have a teachable
spirit. Achievement is sometimes a hindrance to
growth. "I've done this before, I know how to do
this," they say. "I don't need any more training."
Effective leaders don't think that way.
They are eager to grow and learn.*

READ: MATTHEW 5:1-16

*Jim came to serve a small congregation that had a trou-
bled history. Just before he arrived, the board, at the
urging of the denominational leader, had asked the
"church boss" to leave the church. His controlling ways
had kept the church from growing for many years.*

*As the new pastor evaluated the situation, he decided
the greatest need was leadership development. He spent
the first year almost exclusively meeting with and
training the key leaders. A weekly meeting in his home*

built a strong team spirit. Jim met his people at work and occasionally worked with them just to be with them. The chairman confessed that he did not know how to be a board chairman. He did not know how to lead. This pastor's strategy paid off. Within a short time, the church showed signs of health, focused on mission and started reaching the community.

The authors of *The Leadership Baton* say:

Board members are typically well-meaning, but few have ever been mentored for their ministry responsibilities. Rarely has anyone intentionally focused on developing their character, maturity or their theology, especially their theology of the church. Yet they are the most influential leaders in our churches. We have found that most members of governing boards would love to receive leadership training. They long to see their governing experience be more spiritual, effective and enjoyable.

A pastor came to me after one leadership retreat and asked, "So, Abe, how do you train leaders?" Let's begin with Jesus' example, I suggested. He invited His disciples to be with Him, to watch Him, to participate with Him and finally to take over the ministry. He worked Himself out of a job.

1. *It starts with a leader.* People we lead need to see it in us. We need to be the kind of leaders others will seek out, want to be with and follow. We have to have something to give. We will not lead others where we have not been ourselves.

2. *Spend time with your leaders.* Let them see your heart, your passion for the Lord and for the church. See them at their workplace. Ride with them. Go fishing

together. Attend seminars together. With-ness means same-ness.

3. *Invite people to do ministry with you.* Don't work alone. Do visitation with someone. Don't let them just be spectators; encourage them to participate.

4. *Teach.* Jesus spent most of His time with the twelve. He directed most of His teaching at them. Gather good training materials and use them at every opportunity. Take some time at each board meeting to teach about leading.

5. *Empower your leaders.* Give them your blessing. Turn them loose to serve.

When God wanted to bring His people out of Egypt, He raised up Moses to be their leader. When the wall of Jerusalem needed rebuilding, God raised up Nehemiah, calling him out of politics. To prepare for the coming of the Messiah, God raised up John the Baptist.

God always prepared a leader when an important task needed to be done. What is more important today than leading the church of Jesus Christ? A healthy church is the only hope and the best answer to the needs of our hurting world.

Many good people are reluctant to join a leadership team because they don't feel qualified and, once on the board, do not feel qualified to give spiritual leadership. The answer to this need is consistent leadership development.

Do you think that the twelve followers Jesus chose would have met all the leadership qualifications early in their journey? Not a chance. They were very ordinary men, with ordinary weaknesses and failings. Just look at them. They were selfish, and they bickered among themselves just like ordinary people. You know, like board members do at times. But over the three years that Jesus poured His life into them, they grew. They became more like their Master the more time they spent with Him. When the time came for them to assume leadership, they were ready to go. Jesus took three years to prepare His leaders. We need to take our preparation seriously as well.

How can ordinary people in our churches become effective leaders? I think that the answer is in intentionally selecting and training leaders. Perhaps you could go out on a field trip together such as visiting another church that is doing well. You could spend some time sharing with their leadership team. Sometimes our own world is just too small.

When a church is in a constant state of turmoil, the best way out of that cycle and back to health is by refocusing and developing the leaders. As the leaders are, so is the congregation. If your church is facing some very serious difficulties, I suggest that you invite an outside leader to help you. There is a rule that says something like this: "The leaders who got you into this will not likely get you out of it." Don't be afraid to ask for help. Sometimes that is all you can do. Sometimes it is the best thing you can do.

TALK ABOUT THIS:

- How did Jesus prepare the twelve for leadership?
- What activities could help your leadership team right now?
- Do you have access to good leadership materials?

NOW PRAY:

Pray that your leadership team will have a desire to be learning and growing, eager to lead the church to the mission that God has called you to accomplish.

MY NOTES:

"The world is disoriented as to what makes a truly successful leader."

HENRY BLACKABY

Spiritual leadership starts with a servant's heart.

"Only when we understand leadership in light of God's calling on our lives will we be equipped to lead effectively."

HENRY BLACKABY

Genuine leaders walk their talk.

Leaders are learners.

LESSON SIX

The Heart of the Leader

*Effective leadership starts on the inside. It is
what we are that makes us effective. A person
of integrity, who is a growing Christian,
will attract and influence others.*

READ: EXODUS 3:1-14

*Early in my ministry, I was typically concerned about
performing well. I wanted to preach well. I wanted to
give good leadership. I focused primarily on my skills as a
young pastor. A decade into ministry, I began to sense an
inner spiritual hunger. I felt like I was running on my
own energy, like on an empty tank.*

*When a spiritual revival began in one of our
churches, I knew that I needed to be there. God graciously
took me on a new spiritual journey. Serving Him became*

41

a greater joy, something that came from the inside. Ministry was more an overflow from the heart.

The story of Moses' call to serve is especially helpful here. Once before, he had tried to rescue his people, but he did it the wrong way. He tried by force and failed miserably. Forty years later, after a long desert experience, God called him. All of his own dreams and self-confidence had long passed him by. That is when God came and interrupted his life. Then he was ready to follow God's direction. He was ready to serve with God's energy, with heart.

Jesus put it this way when two of the disciples tried to manipulate the system and asked for the top leadership positions: *"The rulers of the Gentiles lord it over them...Not so with you. Instead, whoever wants to become great among you must be your servant"* (Matthew 20:25-26).

Moses also taught us that spiritual leadership is a lifelong learning adventure. He was eighty years old when God called him. A leader who loses that passion has outlived his usefulness. You may have been a leader in your church or in other churches for many years, but you need to keep on growing. We are living in a rapidly changing world. We need to keep abreast of what is happening. The shape of ministry today is such that we need to be lifelong learners. Leaders are learners.

Serving in the church is not just about skills; it's also about heart. It is spiritual work as well. While there are many similarities to leadership in business, there are also important differences. Having a heart for God and for His people is absolutely essential for serving in the church. Bible study and prayer are therefore an essential part of your leadership meetings.

You want to develop your hearts as leaders:

- Make sure that you are walking in fellowship with the Lord. *"Let us fix our eyes on Jesus"* (Hebrews 12:2).
- Maintain an open and honest relationship with your brothers and sisters in the church. *"My command is this: Love each other as I have loved you"* (John 15:12).
- Encourage each other. *"And let us consider how we may spur one another on toward love and good deeds"* (Hebrews 10:24).

Become the kind of people you want your members to become. It was Moses' encounter with God that set him on a new direction to follow and serve Him. That prepared him to serve and to lead from the heart. For forty years, he faithfully led his people, often under very difficult circumstances.

Of all the leadership qualities needed to effectively lead a church, the most important ones are the spiritual qualities. Leading a church is spiritual work and requires that leaders are people of prayer, that they search the Scriptures for guidance and that they are sensitive to the direction of the Holy Spirit.

Keep a healthy balance between learning skills and spiritual preparation of the heart. *The Measure of a Man* is an excellent leadership training book, written by Gene Getz, a pastor in Dallas, Texas. He takes the twenty leadership qualities listed by the apostle Paul in 1 Timothy 3:1-7 and Titus 1:5-10 and develops a short chapter on each one with discussion items and a goal to work on. It's a great learning tool for church leaders.

When we look at the twenty qualifications listed by Paul in his letters, none of us meets all the standards. However, they are a benchmark toward which we all want to and need to grow as leaders. The trouble is that, many times, the benchmark we set is so low that our leadership is not effective. Serving as a leader in a church is a high and honourable calling. We should attract and invite the best to serve.

Leadership training that includes both the heart and skills will build confidence and competence in leaders and inspire new members to join the leadership team.

Jesus was not too concerned about the crowds. His focus was the twelve that He had called to be with Him.

TALK ABOUT THIS:

- Jesus' model of leading was by serving. Does that sound like a contradiction to you?
- Can you relate to Moses' experience? How did you first feel when you were asked to serve on the leadership team?
- What are some ways you can continue to grow as leaders?

NOW PRAY:

Ask the Lord to give you a Christ-like heart for His people. Repent if there is sin in your life. Commit to being a growing Christian leader.

MY NOTES:

Spiritual leadership is a lifelong learning adventure.

Leadership is helping the church achieve its mission.

Leadership is both a gift and a learned art.

"Here is my favorite leadership proverb 'He who thinks he leads, but has no followers, is only taking a walk.'"

JOHN C. MAXWELL

Leaders lead.

There is never a leadership vacuum. Someone will lead.

LESSON SEVEN

About Leading

A church board has the responsibility to ensure that the life of the congregation is healthy and that they are working toward fulfilling their mission.

READ: ACTS 2:40-47

I wondered at times if the "Lakeland Church" would survive. Locked in tradition and bound by conflict, it was stuck and at risk of self-destructing. A church split had left the congregation in serious pain. Reconciliation later brought the two groups back together; however some people had difficulty with all the change that had taken place. There were long and difficult meetings to bring people back together. Gradually, as the pastor began to focus the church on its mission, they started moving forward again. The differences began to melt away, harmony emerged and productive ministry began once again.

Leadership in the town and country church is sometimes challenging. Most are lay led, some by a dominant individual or family. They do not always look to the pastor for leadership. Some don't want a pastor to lead; they would prefer him to be a chaplain who does the marrying, burying and caring.

Some congregations are in states of conflict and disrepair because of problems in their histories. That is most often the result of a lack of qualified leaders. Sometimes they are poorly selected or lack training. Leadership is a learned art. Good leaders don't just appear out of nowhere. They are raised up and nurtured by current leaders who have a vision for the future of the church.

Churches that are in a constant state of tension will burn out their leaders and keep the church from fulfilling its mission. It is sad when a good leader, coming off the leadership team, says, "Never again." Good leadership will help the church focus on vision and mission, not just on itself. A church that is not focusing on mission is not really a New Testament church. It's a social club or something less.

What would be considered an appropriate Christian leadership style in a town and country church? When some people hear "leadership," they assume top-down orders. Our Lord Jesus clearly articulated His philosophy of leadership for His followers in Matthew 20:25-28:

> *You know that the rulers of the Gentiles lord it over them, and their high officials exercise authority over them. Not so with you. Instead, whoever wants to become great among you must be your servant, and whoever wants to be first must be*

your slave—just as the Son of Man did not come to be served,
but to serve, and to give his life a ransom for many.

While the servant model of leadership is appropriate in all Christian circles, it is especially appropriate in the small church, where so much revolves around relationships.

Followership is the fine art of following respectfully when others are leading. It is really just the other side of the leadership coin. Before you can learn to lead, you must learn to follow.

Leadership is not about having your own way as an individual or as a board. Leadership in the Christian context is helping God's people fulfill the mission to which God has called them. In the church, it is to help the church fulfill its mission. It is moving God's people in the direction that He has for them. Egocentric people seek to fulfill their own egos and needs. That is not biblical leadership.

A leader is not always a leader. A mature leader knows when it is appropriate to lead and when it is appropriate to follow. When I am working in my setting or in my ministry, then I am the leader and I lead. When I visit one of our churches, then I am not the leader and I follow, unless I am asked to fulfill some leadership role.

If you are the chair of the board, then that is the setting in which you give leadership. When you are asked to sit in on a committee that has a leader, then you follow. Leadership ebbs and flows. You lead and you follow depending on the need and the role.

The leadership roles between a pastor and the chairman of the board are sometimes a competitive dance. It should not be so. You need to learn to lead when it is appropriate to lead and follow when it is appropriate to follow. Leadership roles should be clearly defined so that each is comfortable with the other.

Some may argue that leadership in the small church is not as important as leadership in the larger church. My answer to that is, it is just as important. However, the leadership model and the style may be different. Even who leads may vary in the small congregation, but leadership is important. Good leadership is imperative.

Some say that there is a leadership vacuum. My view is that there is never a leadership vacuum. Someone will lead. When the right or good people do not lead, bad people will and often with disastrous results. Many church conflicts come out of this scenario.

Who should lead in the town and country church? The biblical model gives the pastor the primary teaching role. Ephesians 4:11-12 says, *"It was He who gave some to be...pastors and teachers, to prepare God's people for works of service, so that the body of Christ may be built up."* Kenneth Wuest, in *Word Studies in the Greek New Testament,* says that a better translation is "pastors who are teachers." They appear to him to be one office or one person.

The primary teacher naturally gives primary leadership as he lays out the teaching of the Bible for the congregation. In most traditions, the pastor is viewed as the head elder, therefore the primary leader. He is, however, not the only elder. Together with the leadership team, however it is constructed, they give leadership to the congregation.

In the small church, it is not always the pastor who is the strongest or the best leader. In fact, some small churches don't really want a pastor to lead. They would like him to be a chaplain who performs the pastoral duties of shepherding, marrying and burying because there is already a long-established leadership person or structure in place.

A long-standing "patriarch" or "matriarch" has sometimes taken the dominant leadership role. Their leadership may be overt or quietly behind the scene as permission givers, but they are the recognized leaders whether they happen to be on the leadership team or not. It gets more complicated if one or two families also dominate this same congregation. A new pastor coming into this situation needs the wisdom of Solomon to understand and work with this congregation.

A pastor who comes into such a church does well to assess the situation before he launches into a major challenge of the status quo. He needs to take time to assess and plan his place. One leader made it a point to build a relationship with the dominant leader and to consult with him about getting things done. Many a pastor has been broken or fired for failing to properly assess the culture of the church before launching into a major offensive.

Let's face it, some of us pastors have not had good leadership training or may not have good leadership skills. Leadership has not always been taught well in the past. Our schools focused on pastoral skills, not on leadership skills. They are different skill sets.

The church board needs to have a good working relationship with the pastor. Expectations need to be clear and up front. In the small church, this is often too informal and seldom talked about. The tragedy is that, by the time any discussion does take place, too much water has gone under the bridge for the relationship to be salvaged.

Expectations need to be spelled out in the letter of call or some document, against which annual reviews may be conducted. If we work hard at this relationship, we will see longer and more fruitful pastorates. Small churches are notorious for not orienting a new pastor to how they do things. It's like there is a conspiracy of silence on these issues—but the pastor better never break any of these unwritten "rules" that they have not explained to him.

Do you agree now that the leadership is an important issue for the town and country church? We must learn the skills of doing small church even better than we are.

Let me say it again: one answer to the challenges of the small church is for a pastor and the leadership team to have regular, ongoing leadership training.

TALK ABOUT THIS:

- What is the biblical leadership model?
- What are the leadership issues in your church right now?
- How could you improve leadership in your church?

NOW PRAY:

Pray that God will guide you as you further develop your leadership team. Pray that the relationship between pastor and board will be healthy. Ask God to give you wisdom in leading your church to fulfill its mission.

MY NOTES:

Leadership is moving God's people in the direction that He has for them.

Followership is the fine art of following respectfully when others are leading.

"Where there is no vision the people perish."

PROVERBS 29:18 KJV

Vision is what drives good leaders.

Leading without vision is like driving from the rearview mirror.

"Christian vision is in short supply."

GEORGE BARNA

LESSON EIGHT

About Mission and Vision

*Christians of vision look at the way things could be
when the church is vital in prayer, devout in
worship, informed in Scripture, and zealous in
mission, and ask—why not?*

–LEITH ANDERSON

READ: NEHEMIAH 2

*Lake Park Baptist Church had been a good, stable,
rural congregation since its beginning in the 1940s.
One problem was that it was fifteen miles off the main
highway on a gravel road and not very accessible to the
larger community. At one leadership meeting, Pastor
Matt Teigrob asked the board what their vision was for
the church.*

*One member responded with, "We need to move our
church." He was asked what he meant. "We need to*

move our church to the main highway," he replied.

Not only did they physically move the church building to the main highway; they added a new auditorium to seat 600 people, all in response to, "What is our vision for our church?" Today they are an effective and growing congregation of 200-plus people, west of the town of Birch Hills, Saskatchewan.

What is our vision? That is the question every church board needs to ask. What is our vision for our church?

Mission and vision—what is the difference? Mission is about the purpose of the church. Why does your church exist? The answer is probably buried deep inside your Constitution. It tells you why your church was organized.

You need to dig it out, dust it off, update it if needed and set it out, framed and posted in a prominent place. You need to keep it in front of you in your leadership meetings. Everything you do and plan should be to fulfill your mission. Are you busy? Busy in itself means nothing. Are you fulfilling your mission? Are you doing what you set out to do? I have seen troubled churches turned around when they began to focus on their mission instead of on themselves.

Vision is how you see your mission developing in the future. What do you want to see happen in your church? What could your church be like five or ten years from now? Ask the question that Pastor Matt asked his board, and see what you can come up with. It could change your church forever.

Vision starts with God. What does He want to see happen here? Listen to God, capture His heart for the church. That begins with prayer. Nehemiah prayed for many months before he came out in the open with his vision for Jerusalem. Praying led Nehemiah to a vision that led him to rebuild the walls of the city of God. He didn't stop until the job was finished.

When you do set out to accomplish a new vision, don't be surprised if you too face opposition, like Nehemiah did. Every worthy cause will be faced with unexpected challenges, sometimes from unexpected sources and, unfortunately, sometimes from our own people.

It's the board's responsibility to develop the vision for and with the congregation. Without vision, we end up just doing maintenance work. Even the small church should have a vision that looks to how it could be, not just what it is now. The mission and the vision of the church should be clear for all to own and support.

To do the planning well, a board needs to hold an annual prayer and planning retreat. A Friday night and all day Saturday at a retreat centre will help you to achieve more than you could in a number of meetings at home. There is never enough time in our regular meetings to do the planning well.

Follow Nehemiah's example. Start with a dream and set out, asking God to guide you as you go forward. He will guide you as you set out to do His will.

TALK ABOUT THIS:

- Look at and discuss the mission of your church.
- Have you ever thought about a vision for your church?
- What is holding you back from moving forward?

NOW PRAY:

Ask God to give you His vision for your church and courage to bring that vision to reality.

MY NOTES:

Mission is about the purpose of the church.
Why does your church exist?

Vision is how you see your mission
developing in the future.
What do you want to see happen in your church?

"But everything should be done in a fitting and orderly way."

1 CORINTHIANS 14:40

The greatest love chapter was directed to the troubled Corinthian church.

What goes on inside the church is more important than what happens around it.

Correction is the most difficult aspect of leadership.

"For God is not a God of disorder but of peace."

1 CORINTHIANS 14:33

Doing Board Better

*Paul wrote the first letter to the Corinthian
believers to bring some order to what had become
chaotic church life. His instructions will guide
your church too.*

READ: 1 CORINTHIANS 1:4-17

*"Abe, why can't we get new people involved in our
church?" Bill asked in a Search Committee meeting.*

*In response, I asked each member of the committee
how long they had been at the church and how long they
had been in leadership. Most of them had grown up in the
church and were long-time leaders.*

*I suggested that perhaps new people saw the friendship
and leadership circles of the church as closed circles and
could not see a way in for themselves. In response to my*

suggestion, they added two members, new to the church, to the Search Committee.

That simple move changed how new people felt about the church. When the new pastor came to The Church on the Prairie, many new people got involved in ministry and on the leadership team.

The first place leaders need to look for guidance is always the Word of God. There are clear imperatives you need to consider. There are examples in the early church that you need to explore. While you must allow for time and cultural differences, there are many important instructions you need to investigate. That is why you will want to spend some time at each meeting to prayerfully search the Scriptures.

Our goal should be to live as close to the Bible as we can. Where God's Word does not give clear guidance, then we adopt the apostle Paul's guideline, to do everything *"in a fitting and orderly way"* (1 Corinthians 14:40). Leaders who prayerfully seek guidance from God and His Word will be an effective leadership team.

Protocol means doing our meetings, our business and our leadership in an orderly way. While every leadership team and every congregation will develop its own "culture" over the years, we need to think about doing "church" and "board" well. The purpose of this lesson is to explore better ways of doing our work as leaders.

Let's start by looking at the board itself.

1. When is a board the board?

Does that sound elementary? First, your board is only the board when you are officially in session together. Once the meeting dismisses, you are simply individual members of the congregation. Individually you do not have board authority.

A meeting in the parking lot by a few after the meeting does not qualify as a legitimate board meeting. That meeting was not officially called or constituted. Any actions taken by a few members would not be legitimate. If a meeting had been called for in the parking lot and members were properly informed, then of course it could be a legitimate meeting. In fact, that could be a good place to meet if you need to plan for more parking.

Secondly, an individual board member cannot speak for the board unless he has been empowered to do so on a specific issue by the board. Individual members do not have authority or board status. The one exception would be that the chairman can speak on behalf of the board if he thinks that he has their support, or in an emergency where someone must speak and take leadership.

If an individual board member has an issue with the pastor, for example, that member can't speak as a member of the board. You can only speak as an individual member of the congregation. He can take his concern to the board, but he does not have board authority outside the board meeting or board empowerment. The pastor can listen, as he should, to his counsel as a member of the congregation, but he does not have to take orders from him just because he is a board member.

2. How long should members serve?

Board members should normally serve for a term of three to four years with one additional term if they are asked.

Failure to bring new leaders in makes for a very ingrown board. Bringing in new leaders also encourages you to keep training new leaders. Furthermore, new people who see a tight leadership team will find assimilation into the church very difficult. New people must see access to friendship, ministry and leadership or they will leave or become inactive in a very short time. Some stay only a month or two.

In very small churches, you may not have the people to rotate leaders. So you do the best that you can with good people. However, the idea of giving everyone a chance to serve on the board is not a wise leadership concept. Some people are not gifted that way and having people on the board who don't have that gift is asking for major problems. Some of the most serious leadership problems that I have had to deal with would fall into this area. Remember that Jesus selected his leaders. He did not ask for volunteers.

3. Diligence and excellence.

Boards need to follow reasonably good leadership and business procedures. Small churches are built around relationships, so use that strength in your meetings. Meetings do not have to be formal, but be careful that you don't get caught without proper procedure, documentation and records.

Decisions can be made by consensus, but they need to be recorded as decisions. I like the consensus model, especially when the leadership team is small. *Robert's Rules of Order* is not a very good model for small churches, but at least it is something to fall back on when needed. A two-page *Summary of Bourinot's Rules of Order* may be more practical for small churches. A copy can be obtained from the author.

When you can't agree on an important business item, perhaps you should postpone the decision, go back to the drawing board and come back later with another, or a more thorough, presentation. Allowing some time for prayerful reflection may allow the Holy Spirit to bring people together.

4. Build consensus.

While you want to work toward consensus on the board, it is not realistic that all board members will agree all of the time. You may have to proceed with one or two negative votes. What happens then? It's not right that one or two members are allowed to dominate the will of the majority. Guard against "bad politics," like behind-the-scenes manipulation, parking-lot decisions and telephone arm-twisting. Discussions should be confined primarily to the board meeting. Remember that you are the board only when you are officially in session.

5. A divided board will divide a church.

You should never bring a divided decision forward to the congregation. You should never say, "The board voted four to three in favour of shingling the roof of the church." A recommendation to the church should represent the entire board. Your motion should read, "The board recommends that...."

A board member who votes against an issue is obligated to support the board once the decision is made. A member can speak against a motion on the board, but he cannot speak against it at the congregational business meeting.

All members must support the board once a decision is made. Members have two options—support the decision or step down from the board. Why? Because a divided board will divide a church. That is a very important leadership principle. You are a leadership team, not a collection of individuals.

6. Issues and personalities.

Church leaders need to learn the fine art of discussing issues without them becoming personal. Never apply motives to members who disagree with you. Don't become too possessive of your own projects and issues. Rejection of an idea is not rejection of the person. Talk ideas not personalities. Take your work seriously, but don't take yourself too seriously. An idea is just an idea—except when it's mine, right?

7. Be an active participant.

Boards need people who will participate in conversation and share their opinions. Just sitting there and being a nice person does not help the board. The board needs alternative and creative ideas. Friction is sometimes helpful, especially if it creates light instead of heat. If two people think exactly alike, one of them is not needed. Healthy boards will debate and challenge ideas.

8. Conflict of interest.

A board member should remove himself from a conflict of interest situation.

> *A board chairman accompanied his pastor to visit a critic. The board member chose not to support the pastor because the critic was a client of his business. He should have told the pastor that he could not go with him on that call because of the conflict of interest. That pastor ended up getting hurt and leaving the church, even though God had used him greatly in the ministry of that church.*

9. Arm's-length.

Arm's-length means that board members do not put themselves in a state of conflict when conducting the business of the church. Having two members from the same family on the board is generally not recommended. When counter-signing cheques and documents, the two signatories need to be unrelated by marriage, family or business interests. An employee of the church, such as the pastor, should not vote on board motions as that puts him in a position of conflict. An example would be him voting on the budget that includes his salary. We need to not only be objective, we must appear to be people of integrity.

I know of one church that had seven brothers on the board. When I questioned the pastor about the advisability of that, his comment was, "I use the best people." That church died a few years later.

10. No surprises, please!

People don't normally like surprises, especially in church business meetings. Most people don't like change. Some seem to think that nothing should ever be done for the first time.

Significant items of business should never be voted on without prior warning and preparation. Governments allow for three readings of a bill in order to invite discussion before the bill is finally passed. A good process for churches is to mention an issue in passing, perhaps in a message or a report. Then place it on the agenda for discussion but no vote. On the third presentation, it is voted on.

Small churches thrive on information and participation by everyone. Church members, however, need to also trust the leaders they elect to make decisions on their behalf. This is a point of tension in small churches. The smaller a church, the more participation the members want.

11. Confidentiality.

Respecting privacy is an important part of a leader's responsibility. Some issues that a church board talks about should stay within the walls of the boardroom. Some things should not even be discussed with a spouse. Sensitive membership issues need to be handled with great sensitivity. While small churches thrive on information about people, there is a confidentiality line that the leaders should not cross. Be especially careful in your prayer requests, as they are sometimes nothing more than an opportunity to share confidential information.

12. Communication.

Providing good information, on the other hand, is tremendously important. A board that seems closed or secretive will not be trusted. You should give regular reports following meetings. Reports can be given verbally by the chairman, printed in the bulletin or in a letter to the members.

You should report things the board is thinking about or actions that they have taken. Pastors should regularly articulate the vision and values of the church so that people are clear on where the leaders are taking the congregation.

Good communication will keep the grapevine thriving on good information. But you won't stop the informal grapevine in the small church or small community. If you fight it, it will simply go underground and cut you off. Learn to use it. It can be an asset. People are talking about the most important thing in their lives—people.

13. What is really most important?

I am sure that we can all agree on this one: the really important issue for the leadership team is discovering and doing the will of God. This is not the board's church—this is God's church. Nothing is more important than finding and doing His will.

Board members need to come to a meeting with an open mind, not with prepared agendas that represent any group or cause in the church—only to seek the Lord's will. The Lord has promised to give you wisdom if you ask (James 1:5).

Leading a church is important spiritual work. When you come to an impasse, stop to pray. Prayer will pull you together. Prayer will empower you, as the Holy Spirit directs you in leading your church.

14. Servant Leaders.

Do more than sit on the board. Serve. Serve your people. Care for hurting members. Pray for the sick, using James 5:13-16 as a pattern. That is a wonderful but neglected ministry. Call on a complaining member, as the complaint may only be an awkward cry for help. People don't call for help very well. Visit new people and visitors to the church. Be a serving leadership team.

TALK ABOUT THIS:

- List some items from this lesson that may need more discussion.
- How could you improve the quality of your meetings?
- Should you plan a leadership retreat to do deeper board work?

NOW PRAY:

Ask God for wisdom as you lead your church. Pray for strength to lead well and with integrity.

MY NOTES:

MORE NOTES:

Leaders who prayerfully seek guidance from God and His Word will be an effective leadership team.

Problems are often disguised as ministry
opportunities.

They are not problems—they are people.

"Paul opposed Peter 'to his face.' That's always
better than opposing someone behind his
back."

BOB BRINER

Leaders must be both strong and tender, like a
velvet-covered brick.

People who don't learn to follow won't learn
to lead.

Solving problems is a part of leadership.

LESSON TEN

Leading Redemptively—
Solving Problems

*A healthy congregation doesn't allow one or two
members to set the church's direction or change
its mission. Neither does it have to enter into
open warfare. Sometimes the answer is
being nice...and firm*

—Marshall Shelly

Read: Galatians 6:1-10

*A pastor in a small town was in trouble because his wife
had disciplined a child in school as a substitute teacher.
Another pastor was fired because the child he disciplined
on a school bus on which he had been the driver was a
friend of a prominent church family. In another church,
one member repeatedly and viciously criticized the pastor
and members of the church without anyone confronting
her about her hurtful behaviour. In another case, I was
called to an urgent meeting by a church board that was*

*meeting in a restaurant to discuss a problem member. I
listened for a while and then asked if they had talked with
this individual. "No," was the answer, "we just want to
talk about it."*

These kinds of problems, characteristic of many small
churches, are very difficult for church leaders to deal with. In
many churches, this kind of dysfunctional behaviour is
allowed to go on, doing great harm to the congregation.

The board needs to have a plan on how to deal with critics
who decide to take a run at the pastor and the leadership of
the church. The pastor and the board should be seen as a team
who lead and serve together. Critics are experts at dividing a
leadership team and playing one side against the other.

Solving problems is part of leadership. Learning to do
that redemptively and graciously is a sign of a mature leadership team. Problems should be seen as opportunities to
grow. They should be viewed as opportunities to help your
people in their spiritual journeys. We are all broken people in
some way. We all need the encouragement that mature
church leaders can give us when we run into trouble.
Learning to solve problems should be part of a leader's
preparation.

Learning to lead redemptively with dissenting people is
an important function of leadership. The Bible instructs us
to be shepherds of God's flock. A shepherd nurtures and
protects. Protecting the congregation is part of leading, but
is sometimes done very poorly. Problems will not go away
left to themselves. You have to care enough to confront. Try
to do it early when the problem is still small.

Criticism is sure to come. It goes with the territory. It is
part of leadership. It will especially come when change is

happening or where God is seen to be at work. It always has been and it always will be so. Let's remember, however, who the real enemy is. You will not please everyone all the time.

Lack of a clear vision may be a cause for unrest. Clarifying the vision will help to refocus the congregation. Indecisive leadership invites challenges. If those in leadership do not lead well, then confusion is created in the congregation and some may rise up to challenge the leaders.

Let me offer a few suggestions on how to deal with a critic.

First, listen to the critic. Sometimes they do have good things to say to us. They may raise issues that our friends are too kind to point out. However, if criticism becomes destructive and malicious, then you have to take action.

Secondly, deal with the critic humbly and redemptively. *"Brothers, if someone is caught in a sin, you who are spiritual should restore him gently. But watch yourself, or you also may be tempted"* (Galatians 6:1).

Thirdly, deal with the critic, and firmly if you have to. *"Warn a divisive person once, and then warn him a second time. After that, have nothing to do with him. You may be sure that such a man is warped and sinful; he is self-condemned"* (Titus 3:10-11). The Holy Spirit cannot bless a church when leaders allow sin to run free (Joshua 7). While only as a last resort, there are times when an individual must be asked to leave the church. An easier way is to help an unhappy person to find another church where they may be happier.

> *Pastor Jim was getting a lot of pressure from Joe, a new attendee, to institute the Lord's supper every Sunday because that is what he was used to in his previous church. Pastor Jim carefully explained that they did it*

once a month and that there was no plan to change that. When the pastor heard that Joe was spreading unrest among the members, he called Joe and suggested that perhaps he should find a church where he could be happy. Joe thought that was a good idea. He called the pastor a few weeks later to report that he found a new church. Where was he attending? He was attending a church that didn't practice communion.

Problems should be dealt with face to face. When a dispute arose in the early church, the leaders in Jerusalem sent a letter to the Gentile church, but with messengers to speak on their behalf *"to confirm by word of mouth what we are writing"* (Acts 15:27). They wrote it down to make sure they got it right, and sent messengers to say it with compassion. That is excellent! A lot of time is wasted in meetings and in relationships because problems are not properly resolved.

The "Calvary" Church board decided to ask one member, who had been a problem for many years, to leave the church. They wrote him a letter that Dave, the chairman, delivered to him in person the next morning. He wept with him and prayed with him, but told him that it was better for the church that he leave. That church turned a corner and became a dynamic and growing congregation.

Leaders need to be good listeners. Constructive criticism should always be welcome. Members should know what the proper procedure is for making a suggestion or filing a complaint. Let's be open and honest about that. Larger churches use a space on the registration card. Others may choose to use a suggestion box. Note paper can be available so notes can be dropped into the offering plate. Verbal communication is of course always best, but however you do it, encourage its use so members feel free to share with their leaders.

However, never read or pass along unsigned letters or notes. They should be destroyed, and members should know that they will not be read. That is not good or fair churchmanship. Policies and procedures like this should be communicated to the congregation and could perhaps be a part of new-member orientation.

> *A pastor found a note waiting for him when he went up to preach. All it said was, "Fool."*
>
> *"Hmm," mused the pastor as he read it out loud. "I have received many letters without signatures, but this is the first signature I have received without a message."*

Where do you set the conduct bar in your church? If leaders allow bad behaviour, then that is where you set the bar. You are then saying, for instance, that it is perfectly fine in this church for anyone to take a run at the pastor, other leaders or fellow members, and this board will do nothing about it. That, my brothers and sisters, is not acceptable. Hear what the Word of God has to say: *"Obey your leaders and submit to their authority. They keep watch over you as men who must give an account. Obey them so that their work will be a joy, not a burden, for that would be of no advantage to you"* (Hebrews 13:17).

Other passages that you will want to study in this context are 1 Timothy 5:17-21 and Matthew 18. This hard work is part of being a leader in the church. If we did just this one thing that Paul admonishes us to do, then we would solve a lot of problems: *"Do not entertain an accusation against an elder unless it is brought by two or three witnesses"* (1 Timothy 5:19). Let's work at this and learn to do it better.

We have many wounded "soldiers" in and around our churches. One of the pains that I carry from doing denominational work is the large number of leaders, pastors and lay, who have left ministry and fail to be involved in leadership again. Some have even left the church. The path of Christian service is littered with broken people and wounded soldiers, many of whom are left to die a slow emotional and spiritual death alone.

Only one pastor in ten who starts out as a young leader actually retires from ministry at age sixty-five, according to Steve Farrar, author of *Finishing Strong*. Church board members get wounded and become discouraged. Let's all work hard at encouraging our leaders so that they can have many years of fruitful service and become happy role models for those who follow them.

TALK ABOUT THIS:

• What are some relational challenges that you are facing right now?
• Are there some relational fences that need mending?
• Is there a problem you have ignored that you need to deal with?
• How can you do redemptive ministry better?

NOW PRAY:

Pray that you will have the grace, the courage and learn the skills to lead those who at times are difficult people in your church.

MY NOTES:

Jesus planned well for His succession.

Each generation faces the challenge of passing the baton on to the next generation.

The church is always just one generation away from extinction.

It takes a leader to raise up another leader.

LESSON ELEVEN

Passing the Torch

*Bringing up new leaders is one of the most
important responsibilities of the current
leadership team.*

READ: ACTS 15:36-16:5; 2 TIMOTHY 2:2

*"Community Fellowship," a church plant with sixty in
attendance, was struggling. The initial core group had
met for about five years but could not break free to grow
to another level. Finally the pastor resigned in frustration
and recommended that they close the church. By the time
I, as the District Minister, was informed what was going
on, it was too late to rally this discouraged group, and the
church closed. This pastor could not see anyone else suc-
ceeding if he could not succeed there.*

I know from first-hand experience what it feels like to leave a ministry that I helped start and gave twenty of my best years to develop. It's not easy and most of us do it poorly. We tend to protect what we start. We get possessive over what we initiate. Many a good ministry has gone down with a founding leader because he could not pass it on to another leader or another generation. While Henry Ford is admired as a great innovator, the Ford Motor Company almost died because the founder could not trust the next generation of leaders.

It is the responsibility of the current leaders to ensure that future leaders are being prepared. Bible schools and seminaries can help, but it has to start in the local church. Yet how many churches give this any serious thought? It is predicted that there will be a shortage of Christian workers in the future. How can we meet that challenge? The answer is right here in the local church leadership team.

We must have the vision and develop the skills to raise up future leaders. Town and country churches have, in the past, been a main source of missionaries and pastors. Let's do it again. Let's do our best to raise up another generation of leaders to help fulfill the Great Commission of our Lord.

Most leaders owe their start to the influence of another leader.

I am very thankful for two pastors who encouraged me to develop my leadership skills. One was Bill Zacharias, a small-town pastor of the church my family attended after we came to faith in Jesus Christ. The other one was Gerald Splinter, a city pastor in Winnipeg, Manitoba, who launched me into full-time ministry.

Dr. Wendell Phillips stated, when young people were asked in a survey why they had not considered ministry, the main response was, "No one asked me." The amazing thing is that when young adults are challenged and given an opportunity, they respond. When Dr. Daryl Busby, president of Canadian Baptist Seminary, called for fifty young adults who would like to explore the possibility of full-time ministry to attend a weekend retreat, he had to turn applicants away, two years in a row.

We need to ensure that the church in the future will be strong and in good hands. New leaders need to be raised up and prepared by the current leaders of the church.

Luke 10 contains a wonderful example of an expanding leadership team. Jesus appointed seventy-two others to go out and preach the good news and then to return and give a report. His plan was assignment, instruction, mission, empowerment and accountability. Multiplying leaders is the best way to expand a ministry.

If the cause of Christ is to continue to go forward, we will need to pay close attention to preparing leaders for the future. How can we do that?

- Pastors can keep an eye on young people and adults who show potential, then encourage and guide them.
- Prospective leaders may be invited to attend a board meeting as part of their training and orientation.
- Invite potential leaders to the annual planning retreat and use part of the retreat to orient and train new leaders.
- Mature leaders can mentor younger leaders one on one.
- The pastor can lead a class for new leaders, such as a breakfast where potential leaders are taught skills.
- The current leadership team can make room for new leaders and pass the baton on to them.

Preparing new leaders is one of the greatest needs in the church today.

TALK ABOUT THIS:

• How long has it been since you have brought new leaders on to your leadership team?
• Are there some younger leaders in your church that you need to encourage?
• Talk about how you can develop new leaders.

NOW PRAY:

"Ask the Lord of the harvest...to send out workers into his harvest field" (Matthew 9:38).

MY NOTES:

It is the responsibility of the current leaders to ensure that future leaders are being prepared.

Jesus called us to greater commitment than the rest of the world does.

Raise the standard and good people will respond.

"Some call it stubbornness; I call it principled leadership."

RUDOLPH GIULIANI
FORMER NEW YORK MAYOR

Make plans by seeking advice.

PROVERBS 19:2

LESSON TWELVE

Doing It Right— Legal Matters

*The proverb says it's "the little foxes that ruin
the vineyards" (Song of Solomon 2:15).
Often it's the little things that get us into trouble.
It's often not the big things that members are
critical about—it's the small things that irritate
like a little pebble in your shoe.*

READ: MATTHEW 5:13-20

*The "Church in the Village" had a rather narrow focus
on ministry. A division resulted in some years of pain
and conflict. Reconciliation later brought the two
groups back together. It took half-a-dozen years of hard
negotiation to work out the wrinkles and bring peace
and focus to the church. They had to learn new ways of
doing church. It was like starting over but with some
old traditions hanging on. New people had to be assim-
ilated. A number of times, it came close to falling*

apart altogether. With patient teaching and strong leadership, the church gradually found its mission again, with more vigour than ever before.

The Sermon on the Mount (Matthew 5) was our Lord's manifesto. Here He laid out the principles of His Kingdom. In this passage, He reminds us that the world is watching. He told us that we are "salt" by the life we live and "light" by the words we speak. It is therefore important that we conduct our lives in such a way that we are a positive example, and that includes how we conduct the business of our church. Not only should our individual lives reflect the values of His Kingdom, our corporate lives, too, must reflect His values in this dark and chaotic world.

Missionary friends were taking my wife and me on a tour of Mexico City. We noticed a Baptist church with a chain and padlock on the front door. We were told that, because of ongoing conflict in the church, the government decided to lock it up. All church buildings in Mexico are the property of the government. Not a great witness to a watching world, is it?

While a church is a divine organism, it is also a legal organization. It is the responsibility of the board to see that important legal matters are cared for properly. That comes under the biblical category of everything being *"done in a fitting and orderly way"* (1 Corinthians 14:40).

Legal matters may not be at the top of the list of our responsibilities as boards; nevertheless, they are important. It has been said by people in the Canadian Council of Christian Charities that the average church does enough illegal things that the government could, if it wanted to, come in at any time and shut it down. They don't because it is not in their best interest. They recognize too that churches are largely volunteer-run organizations and that they provide a valuable service to their communities.

However, that is no excuse for doing things poorly. We are not being a good example to the world if we conduct our business in an irresponsible manner.

Most denominations have personnel and programs that can assist congregations with charitable and legal matters. Your church can benefit from their services. Small churches have a tendency to isolate themselves and struggle on alone. Struggling churches, like people in pain, will seldom reach out for help. Make use of the good resources that are available to you.

Who needs a Constitution? How many times have I heard, "O, we don't go by the Constitution." Every church needs their Constitution. It is important. This is a legal document and allows the congregation to function as a legal entity. This document should be kept current and relevant. A good Constitution can save a church in a time of crisis. Constitutions and Bylaws should serve the church but not be its master. I wonder how many board members have read their Constitution and Bylaws? It should be part of every new leader's orientation.

Proper forms required by the government need to be filed regularly, as required for both the province and the Revenue Canada agency that allows the church to issue receipts for charitable donations. Regulations vary from province to province, and some provinces do not require churches to register.

In Canada, it is not legal for pastors who are deemed to be employees of the church to be voting members of the board. That is considered to be a conflict of interest. While the practice varies in different denominations, in mine, the board is an autonomous entity and the pastor serves as an ex-officio member. My view is that a pastor does not need to be a voting member of the board to give good leadership.

The board's relationship with the pastor needs to be carefully maintained. This is a very special relationship. Like any good relationship, it takes time and hard work. The best time to clarify expectations is when you call a new pastor. It would be a good idea to write these things down and to review and renegotiate them annually. Too many pastors are being hurt. While it is true that it is the pastor's responsibility to care for the church, it is also true that it is the church's responsibility to care for their pastor. The board needs to give positive leadership here.

Churches are very vulnerable because they rely on volunteers. Everyone serving in the church needs to be given proper training and coaching. Members should not be put into vulnerable situations where they can get hurt unnecessarily.

Areas to which a board needs to pay special attention:

- Clarify roles and expectations with the pastor;
- Keep the relationship with the pastor healthy;
- Keep the Constitution and Bylaws current and relevant;
- Institute policies instead of micro-managing;
- Give proper notice of meetings;
- Develop job expectations for ministry leaders;
- Institute a policy to protect children and volunteers;
- Develop procedures for handling money;
- Ensure that payroll and deductions are carefully managed;
- Make sure that receipting of charitable gifts is properly carried out;

- Make sure that required reports to governments are done on time;
- Ensure that privacy legislation is instituted; and
- Handle conflict biblically and with grace.

Does this sound a little onerous and complicated for a small church? I'm sure it does, but we are living in a complicated world. Some of these items, however, are not small. Some of them, if not managed well, could put a church out of business. Lawsuits against churches are becoming more common. Where our witness is at stake, it is important.

Talk About This:

- Who looks after the administration of your church?
- What are some things that need your attention?
- Are there some issues for which you should get outside help?
- Are you familiar with resources that could help you?

Now Pray:

Ask the Lord to protect your church from incidents that could hurt your church and harm your witness in your community. Pray for those people in your church who handle funds, who work with children and others who serve in high-risk ministries.

My Notes:

MORE NOTES:

It has been said by people in the Canadian Council of Christian Charities that the average church does enough illegal things that the government could, if it wanted to, come in at any time and shut it down.

"The earth is the LORD's and everything in it."

PSALM 24:1

Stewardship is the gospel for a materialistic
society.

Financial maturity is giving up today's desires
for tomorrow's benefit.

"All the believers were one in heart and mind.
No one claimed that any of his possessions
was his."

ACTS 4:32

LESSON THIRTEEN

Money—A Slippery Slope

*Stewardship is the idea that God owns everything,
that we are His managers, caring responsibly for the
resources that He has entrusted to us individually
and to our church corporately.*

READ: 1 CORINTHIANS 16:1-4

*"Daisy" had been a faithful church member for many
years. Valley Church was like her second family. She had
been the church treasurer for more years than she could
remember, and taking care of the money was her special
task. That she was trusted was evident in that she not only
was the treasurer, she also counted the money—alone,
deposited it—alone, wrote the cheques—alone and gave
the financial reports—alone.*

While no one had ever questioned Daisy about any

*irregularity, she was, without knowing it, in a very vul-
nerable situation. If anyone ever challenged her, she
would have no witnesses and no way of defending herself.*

Paul was concerned that the money be handled responsibly and that it appeared to be handled properly. The proper
handling of funds is a challenge in every church. Failure to
do so has been the ruin of some churches and the downfall
of many a leader.

When people were asked in a survey why they did not
attend church, the number-one reason given was that all the
church wanted was their money. While we know that is not
true, this perception is nevertheless very damaging.

Boards lose trust and credibility faster on money matters
than almost any other issue in the church. Remember, in the
end, it is the board that is responsible. I would not serve on
a church board if financial matters were handled poorly.
Board members are liable. For this reason, many boards now
carry liability insurance, and that is expensive.

Financial books need to be audited or reviewed by an
impartial individual, a committee or an accounting firm on
an annual basis, prior to the annual meeting. This has to be
done well and appear to be done well. It also serves to protect the people involved. That, too, is important. The fee to
have it done professionally is a good investment, although
not required.

Biblical stewardship education should be part of a
church's ongoing education. An annual sermon on giving is
not enough. Good resources that include children and
youth are available and should be part of your library of
resources or borrowed from other churches or from your
denomination.

Some small churches often don't want a pastor to talk about money, as if it's not spiritual or it's out of his realm of responsibility. It's everyone's responsibility, especially the leadership team's. Lyle Schaller, one of my favourite writers, said in a seminar I attended, "I will tell you how to raise the level of giving in a church. Let the pastor tithe and not keep it a secret. Let every deacon tithe and not keep it a secret."

Example is worth more than a dozen good sermons. I believe that every member of the leadership team should be required to tithe their income, *"to make ourselves a model for you to follow"* (2 Thessalonians 3:9). I think it is a conflict of interest not to support the cause that you speak for and serve.

While I say this with some caution, I have a hunch that most criticism comes from people who are not giving sacrificially to the church. I once saw a group of critics leave a church. The offering the following Sunday had not dropped a dime. A friend of mine, John Bergeson, used to say, "Most criticism comes from the cheap seats." I think that it is good leadership when the board chair gets up before the people to report and give appeals when needed, but he must have credibility. People know when it does not ring true.

Financial problems are sometimes a symptom of other needs. When members are unhappy, they will often withhold giving as a form of protest. Wise leaders will use this thermometer to look deeper and solve needs instead of focusing on a symptom.

A budget is a church's statement of values. It tells you what is important to your church. In that sense, it is the most important item on your annual meeting agenda. Does it reflect your church's vision? In the small church, preparing the budget is often done very informally. You need to give it careful thought and prayer.

While most churches struggle with enough income, small churches often face some tough choices. "Do we pay the fuel bill, or does the pastor get paid this month?" Some may have to choose a bi-vocational pastor or link up with another small congregation to share a pastor.

One of the most difficult things for any church is to cut back when the population and congregation decline. It can be very demoralizing. Ask for outside help to work through these hard issues. Don't struggle alone, and by all means, don't feel guilty when you cannot change the circumstances. Try to keep a spiritual light shining in the community, even if it is just a home Bible study.

> *A pastor announced that he had good news and bad news. With great enthusiasm, he told the congregation that the Lord had provided all the funds needed for their new building program.*
>
> *There was much rejoicing and applause, until one gentleman dared ask, "And Pastor, what is the bad news?"*
>
> *"The bad news," replied the pastor with some hesitation, "is that the money is still in your wallets and purses."*

The Bible has much to say about money. Jesus said more about money than about love, faith, prayer or heaven. Money is much on His mind because He knows that it is much on ours.

TALK ABOUT THIS:

- What financial challenges are you facing as a church?
- How do you feel about leaders setting the pace in giving?

- Do you have any weak spots in money-handling procedures?
- How can you improve the stewardship education in your church?

NOW PRAY:

Thank God that He holds all the wealth of this world and that He is the one who supplies your needs. Thank Him for the faithful givers in your church and ask Him to supply your needs right now.

MY NOTES:

Organization is like the skeleton of the body, not visible but supportive.

Keep structures simple but not too simple.

Just because you are small does not mean you can't be good.

LESSON FOURTEEN

Keep the Organization Healthy

*While the church is much more than an
organization, it is still an organization and
needs to be well cared for to be healthy.
An unhealthy organization can sometimes
be the cause of spiritual problems.*

READ: ACTS 6:1-7

Listen to a tale of two churches. Both are rural, small-town churches. One is growing while the other is declining. "Prairie Church" decided that they were not well positioned in the community and chose to relocate to a more prominent location. As a result of this renewed vision, they began to attract new people and the church grew remarkably.

"Village Church," on the other hand, has seen their congregation and community decline steadily, with

little hope of new growth taking place. Their long-term survival is uncertain.

Two town and country churches with very different futures. Yet, remarkably, they have one thing in common. The structure and organization that once served them well is no longer meeting their needs. One is over-organized because of decline, while the other one needs new structures and more organization because of the growth it is experiencing.

The early church experienced explosive growth. The complaint that some widows were not being cared for highlighted a need. So, thank God for complaints, right? The complaint alerted the leaders to the needs of their growing church. How they responded is a wonderful example for us.

"Dan" was a gifted young pastor and "Community Church" was growing at a healthy rate. When a founding couple came to him and complained that all he cared about was new people, Dan panicked and shifted his focus from reaching and discipling new people to caring for older members. The growth stopped and the church has struggled ever since.

The Apostles did not abandon their priorities to meet an important need. Instead, they multiplied the leadership team members and empowered them to meet that need, while they maintained their primary focus. It's easy for leaders to lose their focus under pressure. The Apostles expanded the organization and leadership so that they could stay focused on their mission—prayer and preaching.

Organization and structure are not necessarily biblical or legal matters but they are nevertheless important. The structure of a church is like the skeleton of the human body. It is never visible but soon becomes apparent if it is not strong enough to support the body. The structure does not give it life; it helps to support the life. Some churches suffer from an organizational osteoporosis.

Structures and organization should reflect the mission and the size of the church. Small churches are often over-organized. That may be a carry-over from former days when they were a larger church. A small board of three qualified leaders can very well serve a small congregation. The person who loses fifty pounds has to buy a new suit of clothes. In the same way, churches outlive their organization and structure.

A growing congregation needs to upgrade its organization, or it will become restrictive. The structure and organization should reflect the current realities of the church. Organization should be a servant not a master.

One board is enough for any size church. I believe strongly in a one-board structure. My home church has more than 1,200 in attendance on Sunday morning, and it has only one board. Yet some small churches of fewer than fifty people have two boards. In my opinion, two boards are a prescription for conflict in leadership. One board, the size of which should reflect the size of the church, with sub-committees or teams, is all that is needed. In very small churches, individuals can be assigned to certain tasks instead of appointing committees. It is more important that people serve than that they sit on boards and committees.

Albert Einstein is not known for being an expert on churches, but what he said can apply: "Try to keep it as simple as possible, but not simpler."

When things like job expectations, policies and guidelines for officers and leaders of ministries are clearly laid out, they help to make the church run smoothly. You don't want them to be restrictive but, rather, empowering. Spiritual leadership is about empowering people to serve not about controlling them or the ministry of the church.

While not at the top of the list, keeping the organization of the church healthy is still a very important matter for a church board. Let's do it well.

TALK ABOUT THIS:

- Are there needs in your church that are not being met currently?
- How does your church compare today to ten years ago?
- What changes may help your church to be more effective?

NOW PRAY:

Ask the Lord to guide you in providing the structure and the people so that as leaders you can keep your priorities to help your church to fulfill its mission.

MY NOTES:

"Try to keep it as simple as possible, but not simpler."

ALBERT EINSTEIN

There is no success without a successor.

The church is always just one generation away
from extinction.

Leadership is not about control—it's about
empowering others.

Stepping aside graciously to allow new leaders
in is a sign of spiritual maturity.

LESSON FIFTEEN

Know When to Step Aside

*There is a time for all of us leaders to step aside
and make room for new and younger leaders
to take our place. Few of us do that well.*

READ: JOSHUA 1:1-9

*After twenty years of leading a ministry that I had
helped to start, I knew the time would come for me to
step aside. I wanted to do that before I was either asked
to leave or could no longer keep up the pace of our
growing ministry. I began reading on the subject and
talking to people who had done it well. I discovered that
it would take some very intentional planning and good
decisions to make a gracious exit. I had to set the good
of the ministry ahead of my own feelings. It would take*

humility on my part. By God's grace, I can say that the transition to a new leader has gone well.

God called Moses "home" to get him out of the way. A new era had come. A new generation needed to be led into a new adventure. A new leader was therefore needed. No one questioned the great contribution that Moses had made, least of all Joshua. Even today, Moses is honoured as one of history's greatest leaders. But he was a man of his time and needed to make way for a new leader. One of Moses' greatest acts was to mentor and encourage Joshua, who would become his successor.

Leaders are people of their time, and times change. Few leaders are willing or able to change enough to lead into the future. God calls and brings new leaders forward to take His church to the next level and the next generation.

Joshua teaches us to honour leaders that God has put in place and to wait for our turn to lead. Sometimes church members manipulate themselves into places of leadership. Remember that it is the Lord who gave leaders to the church (Ephesians 4:11) and He still does that today.

I have seen churches torn apart by leaders who refused to step aside.

"Calvary Church" had an effective ministry but was reduced to twenty people by one man who had controlled the church for years. When he disagreed with the pastor over a minor issue, he forced the pastor out and nearly destroyed the church in the process. It took many years for the church to recover.

I fear for such people, for they will be judged by God one day for these terrible deeds against His people—not to mention the poor testimony that it is to the community (2 Corinthians 5:10).

Leaders normally protect what they start. When change threatens their leadership, they often take it as a personal affront to their achievements and credibility. Sometimes they get too possessive about the church. It's not ours, after all, is it? It is the church of Jesus Christ.

I have seen God move or remove key people, like He did Moses, in order to make way for new people and new leaders to get involved.

A small-town church had a very gifted man in leadership. "John" was also a prominent leader in the community. Many looked to him for leadership. When the income fell short at the end of the year, no one worried because John would make it up.

The young pastor was quite intimidated by John's leadership and teaching abilities, especially when John suggested that the pastor was not that good a preacher. In order to encourage the pastor, the regional leader met with John, who was a friend of his, and suggested that perhaps he could be a little more encouraging to his young pastor.

John was so offended that he sold his business and moved out of town. The interesting thing was that the church began to grow. While John didn't do it intentionally, he had been stifling the church.

It's a sad picture to see angry former leaders standing around and criticizing the current leaders. Jim, one of the younger leaders in one church, told me that it's really hard for young leaders to have the older, more "mature" members criticizing them all the time. Older people, especially older leaders, need to be encouragers of the younger and the new leaders. Those of us who move on need to find new forms of ministry, perhaps mentoring younger leaders. We should be the first to encourage them. Christian leadership is not about controlling but about empowering others to serve.

There are distinct advantages to rotating leaders. New people bring fresh ideas and new energy. New people to your church must be able to see a way into the friendship circles, into ministry and into leadership. If they don't, they become inactive in a very short time, or they simply leave.

Assimilating new people into smaller churches is one of their greatest challenges. Keeping the same people in key leadership positions may close the door for new people to come in.

If, as a small church, you don't have enough leaders to rotate them, you need to just do the best you can with the good people that you have.

TALK ABOUT THIS:

- How successful are you at welcoming and assimilating new people?
- Do you bring new people into leadership positions?
- Do you have a plan to train new leaders?
- How do you honour and use leaders who come off the board?

NOW PRAY:

Ask God to give you the grace to be an inclusive leadership team. Pray that God will bring new people to your church and help you to raise up new leaders. Pray too for wisdom to know when to step aside and make way for others to take your place.

MY NOTES:

Moses had assumed total responsibility for judging the disputes of three million people. Jethro reprimanded Moses for poor management. Always be willing to accept sound advice—even from your in-laws.

Moses was told to "select capable men." Not just anyone will do when you delegate responsibility.

EXODUS 18:21

Assign people tasks that are equal to their capabilities.

LESSON SIXTEEN

Being the Board Chair

The board chair is without doubt the most important position on the board. He sets the tone for the meetings, gives appropriate leadership and helps the board achieve its objectives.

READ: EXODUS 18

"I don't know how to be a chairman," "Dave" confessed in a meeting. "I don't know how to lead." I have heard that statement more than once in consulting with churches. In Dave's case, it was not inability on his part, but that he had not been empowered to lead. Someone else was manipulating people behind the scenes. When empowered to do so, Dave became a very gifted leader.

Being the leader of a team of leaders is very different than leading a ministry in the church. It's different than working alone or being a member of a team. You have to start thinking differently. You have to think like a leader. You have to see the big picture. You have to think ahead—you have to anticipate the future and be prepared for anything to happen. You have to keep cool even when everyone around you is in turmoil.

Moses had been tending sheep. That is what he knew best. What he learned from his father-in-law was how to lead shepherds, not sheep. There is a big difference.

As chair of the leadership team, you too are leading a team of leaders. Follow Moses' example, and you will have good success as a team leader.

Team leaders should be carefully chosen and have the following qualifications:

- Be a person of solid character;
- Have the ability to lead;
- Be respected by his peers;
- Be willing to lead by example;
- Have a genuine commitment to the church;
- Be a team player;
- Have the good of the leadership team at heart; and
- Be able to work productively with the pastor.

The board chair and the pastor must have a good working relationship. They need to respect each other and both have the good of the church as their objective. Their relationship will reflect how things go in the church. The chairman should not compete with the pastor for leadership. Roles for both should be clear. You must work together for the good of the congregation. A divided leadership will divide the congregation.

Who does what?

While there is variation in each situation because of personality and gifting, the pastor, being the shepherd of the congregation, will look after the spiritual welfare of the flock. He has the primary teaching and preaching role and, therefore, will most naturally give overall leadership to the church. He helps to develop the vision. By his example, he leads in evangelism and the outreach of the church. He has the primary responsibility of developing the leaders and helping the church fulfill its mission. He works closely with and helps to build the leadership team.

The board chair leads the board and helps the board to fulfill its objectives and the mission of the church. The chair helps the board develop policies and uphold the Constitution and Bylaws. The chair sees that members are trained and helps prepare new members to take their place. Together, they care for the pastor and make sure that the relationship with the pastor is a happy and productive one.

Prepare well for your meetings.

The chair should meet with the pastor prior to a board meeting to prepare the agenda. He should ask the pastor how he is doing in his ministry and if the board can support or help him in any way. If there is a parsonage involved, there are often concerns around maintenance and privacy that the board should be aware of. Make sure that you review his salary and that you talk about the issues of compensation at least on an annual basis. A paper entitled *Caring for Your Pastor* is available from the author free of charge. Focus on the Family has some material for an annual pastor-appreciation event. It is a well-established fact that longer pastorates are more productive ministries.

Your agenda should include the following:

1. A short time at the beginning to let members visit. Members who have something they need to talk about will not be focused on the business. They may as well get it out first. Small churches are built around relationships, so use that strength in your meetings.
2. A devotional from God's Word given by the chairman or as assigned, and an opening prayer.
3. Board training.
4. The pastor's report.
5. Talk about what is happening in the church.
   - What good things are taking place?
   - Are any needs coming forward that you should know about? This discussion may lead to some additional business items.
6. Special reports.
7. Review the minutes of the last meeting.
8. Review and adopt the agenda.
9. The business.
10. Closing prayer time for the church and its ministries. Don't rush. Prayer is an important part of your work. A brief closing prayer is hardly what is called intercession.

A leader leads.

- Be the first to arrive at the meeting. It frustrates members to wait for their leader.
- Select the meeting place carefully. Small stuffy rooms are not conducive to good meetings. The environment contributes to the attitude of a meeting. I would rather meet in a gymnasium than in a small room. A congested meeting place does not foster vision.

- Meet around tables large enough so that you are not crowded and so that every member is clearly visible and able to participate. Two long tables formed into a square is a good setting.
- If copies of the agenda have been handed out prior to the meeting, make sure that you still bring extra copies for each member. Place a copy of the agenda and a glass of water for each member, with an extra pitcher of water on the table. A dish of mints or nuts may add a nice touch.
- Make sure you understand your Constitution and Bylaws and have copies available at the meetings.
- Pray about the meeting. Ask God to guide you and to guide the board. God's business is always important business. It's the most important business in the world.

Leading the meeting.
- As chair, you should view your role as the moderator of the meeting.
- Your job is to help your leadership team fulfill its responsibilities and achieve the purpose of the meeting and mission of the church.
- Orient new members to the board. Make them feel that this is really important and that their time and gifts are appreciated and needed.
- Make sure that all members participate. Watch so that the talkers don't dominate the meeting. Go around the table for views on matters, or say, "I'd like to hear what Bill has to say on this issue."
- Keep your own opinions to a minimum, at least until others have voiced theirs. This is not about you get-

ting your way but about the leadership team finding God's way.

- Stick to the topic. Call members back to the topic if necessary. If important other issues arise, list them for discussion later, but don't let the meeting run off on rabbit trails.
- Learn to discuss issues without making them a personal campaign.
- Never question someone else's motives.
- Make sure that a secretary is in place and that there is a good record of the meeting. Minutes should include the following:
  - Members who are present and absent.
  - Record of motions and decisions verbatim.
  - In addition to the decisions, list some of the conversation surrounding the decision. You should be able to go back to the minutes later and understand how the meeting and business developed.
  - Attach copies of the agenda and reports to the minutes.
- Both the chair and the secretary should sign the master copy of the minutes.
- Make copies of minutes available to all members as soon as possible so that decisions can be carried out.
- In addition to the minutes, you should develop a policy manual. Developing carefully thought-out policies is more important than micro-managing everything and everybody.
- Confirm ahead of time that any members who are to bring reports or have assignments are present and prepared.

Small boards find formal motions cumbersome.

Try making decisions by consensus. After some discussion, you can ask, "Are we agreed then that…(give your summary of the discussion)…?" The minutes should then read, "It was agreed that…."

If you cannot get a consensus, perhaps you should delay a decision, especially on important issues, until the next meeting, to allow members to think about the matter or to do more research and preparation. You may, at times, have to move on an issue with someone in disagreement, but try to get the dissenter to support the decision in the end.

On important issues or legal matters, you should pass a motion and have it seconded and voted on.

Find ways to enhance your meetings and keep them interesting.
- Set a time limit on meetings. Ask members how much time they have and set a time to end the meeting. Meetings should never go beyond 10.00 p.m. Nothing much good happens after that time.
- Talk about how your meetings can improve.
- Be creative. Move the meeting to different places. Hold a meeting around dinner or lunch in a restaurant or a home.
- Make sure you have an annual overnight retreat once a year.
- Go on a field trip to visit another church that is doing well and meet with their board to see how they do things.
- Equip your members to be the best they can be. Watch a video together. Share some ideas from a book.

- Be a learner. Leaders are readers. Sharpen your skills as a leader. Keep growing.

TALK ABOUT THIS:

- Are members feeling fulfilled serving on the board?
- How can you keep your meetings interesting and effective?
- What can you do to keep on learning and growing?

NOW PRAY:

Ask God to guide your leadership team in helping your church to fulfill the mission to which God has called you. Ask members to pray for you as the chair of the board.

MY NOTES:

...And To Wrap This Up

Many of us can identify with Peter, a follower of Jesus and leader in the early church. While he followed enthusiastically, he also failed and fumbled at key moments. It was only after the Lord's patient encouragement that he considered coming back after he so blatantly denied the Lord in His greatest moment of need.

I can think of many times when I behaved as badly as Peter did. It reminds me over and over that God does not use me because of who I am but only by His grace and His Spirit in me. This is His work, not mine. I can only follow Him and ask Him to use me. Without Him, I can do nothing. On the other hand, with Him I can do all things. Like Rick Warren says, in *The Purpose Driven Life*, "It's not about you."

The church is His. I am only a servant. He has not asked us to be successful, only to be faithful. We can do that, can we not?

Peter's encouragement to us as fellow leaders is this: *"But grow in the grace and knowledge of our Lord and Savior Jesus Christ. To him be glory both now and forever"* (2 Peter 3:18).

Some Valuable Resources

Shepherding the Small Church, Glenn Daman, Kregel Books

No Little Places, Klassen and Koessler, Baker

Making the Small Church Effective, Dudley, Abingdon

Small Churches are the Right Size, David R. Ray, Pilgrim Press

The Purpose Driven Church, Rick Warren, Zondervan

Setting the Church Free, Neil T. Anderson, Regal Books

Spiritual Leadership, Blackaby, Broadman and Holman

Leading and Managing the Church, Carl George/Robert Logan, Fleming H. Revell

The 21 Irrefutable Laws of Leadership, John Maxwell, Thomas Nelson

The Leadership Baton, Forman, Jones and Millar, Zondervan

Developing the Leaders Around You, John C. Maxwell, Thomas Nelson

Leading Your Church to Growth, Peter Wagner, Regal Books

Transitioning, Dan Southerland, Zondervan

Caring for Your Pastor, Abe Funk

Pastors at Risk, H. B. London, Neil B. Wiseman, Victor Books

Stewardship; Crown Ministries, Longwood Florida

Legal and Financial; Canadian Council of Christian Charities

Credits

LESSON ONE
Michael Griffiths, *Cinderella with Amnesia*, Inter-Varsity Press
Ray C. Stedman, *Body Life*, Regal Books
Rick Warren, *Purpose Driven Life*, Zondervan

LESSON TWO
Carl S. Dudley, *Small Churches are the Right Size*, Abingdon
Lyle Schaller, *The Small Church is Different*, Abingdon

LESSON THREE
Christian A. Schwarz, *The ABC's of Natural Church Development*, The International Centre for Leadership Development and Evangelism

LESSON FOUR
J. Robert Clinton, *The Making of a Leader*, NAVPRESS
John C. Maxwell, *Developing the Leaders Around You*, Thomas Nelson Publishers

Fred Smith, *Learning to Lead*, The leadership Library, Word Books

Sir Ernest Shackleton, *Our Daily Bread*, RBC

LESSON FIVE

Rowland Forman, Jeff Jones and Bruce Miller, *The Leadership Baton*, Zondervan

LESSON SIX

Henry and Richard Blackaby, *Spiritual Leadership*, Broadman and Holman

Gene Getz, *The Measure of a Man*, Regal Books

LESSON SEVEN

Kenneth Wuest, *Word Studies in the Greek New Testament*, Eerdmans

Leith Anderson, *Dying for Change*, Bethany House

John C. Maxwell, *21 Irrefutable Laws of Leadership*, Thomas Nelson Publishers.

LESSON EIGHT

Leith Anderson, A quote from a message

George Barna, *The Power of Vision*, Regal Books

LESSON TEN

Marshall Shelley, *Well-Intentioned Dragons*, The Leadership Library, Word Books

Bob Briner, *Men in Leadership*, Holman Reference

Steve Farrar, *Finishing Strong*, Multnomah Books

Order Form

HOPE FOR THE SMALLCHURCH

(Please Print)

Name _____

Address _____

Town/City _____ Prov/State _____

Postal Code/Zip_____ Phone _____ - _____

Email _____

_____ Copies @ Canadian $12.95, U.S. 10.95

Please add $3.00 postage for first book – and $2.00 for
each additional book.   /. 50

Amount enclosed $ _____

You may pay by check or Postal Money Order payable to
Abe Funk

Please send orders to:
Abe Funk, #27 – 308 Jackson Road NW,
Edmonton, AB T6L 6W1
Phone 780-466-6244
Email: abefunk@shaw.ca

About the Author

In 2002, Abe Funk concluded forty-seven years of active and full-time ministry. Prior to his retirement, he was the national leader of the Baptist General Conference of Canada, a ministry that he helped organize in Canada. He served in that capacity for eighteen years.

He married Ann in 1958, the same year that they began ministry together. They have always worked together as a team. Abe and Ann have two children and three grandchildren. They make their home in Edmonton, Alberta, Canada.

Abe grew up on a farm in southern Saskatchewan. His first church experience as a new believer was in a small-town church where a fine pastor mentored him and allowed him to experiment with ministry and leadership.

He began his education in a one-room country school, and continued at Briercrest High School and Swift Current Bible Institute. Continuing education has been his lifelong passion. In 2001, the Canadian Baptist Seminary, part of the Associated Canadian Theological Schools at Trinity Western

University in Langley, BC, granted Abe an honorary Doctor of Divinity degree.

His ministry began with a pastorate in Minnesota. Abe and Ann then directed an evangelism outreach team, travelling with thirty-five young people for seven years all over the United States and Canada. Coming back to Canada in 1966, they planted a new church in White Rock, BC.

Abe is currently serving as part-time District Minister in Saskatchewan, mentoring pastors and coaching churches, the majority of which are town and country churches. It is from this ministry that the material in this book first came together. He has used it to help some struggling churches get on the road to health and effectiveness.

His goal for the long term is to write as God gives him the opportunity.